ABOUT THE AUTHOR

Neil Ardley has written a number of innovative nonfiction books for children, including *The Eyewitness Guide to Music*. He also worked closely with David Macaulay on *The Way Things Work*. In addition to being a well-known author in the fields of science, technology, and music, he is an accomplished musician who composes and performs both jazz and electronic music. He lives in Derbyshire, England, with his wife and daughter.

Project Editor Laura Buller
Editor Bridget Hopkinson
Art Editor Christopher Howson
Production Catherine Semark
Photography Pete Gardner

Library of Congress Cataloging-in-Publication Data
Ardley, Neil.
The science book of gravity/Neil Ardley.—1st U.S. ed.
p. cm.
"Gulliver books."
Summary: Simple experiments demonstrate the laws of gravity.
ISBN 0-15-200621-4
1. Gravitation—Juvenile literature. 2. Gravity—Measurement—Experiments—Juvenile literature.
[1. Gravity—Experiments. 2. Experiments.] I. Title.
QC178.A65   1992
531'.14—dc20   92-3413

Reproduced in Hong Kong by Bright Arts
Printed in Belgium by Proost
First U.S. edition 1992
A B C D E

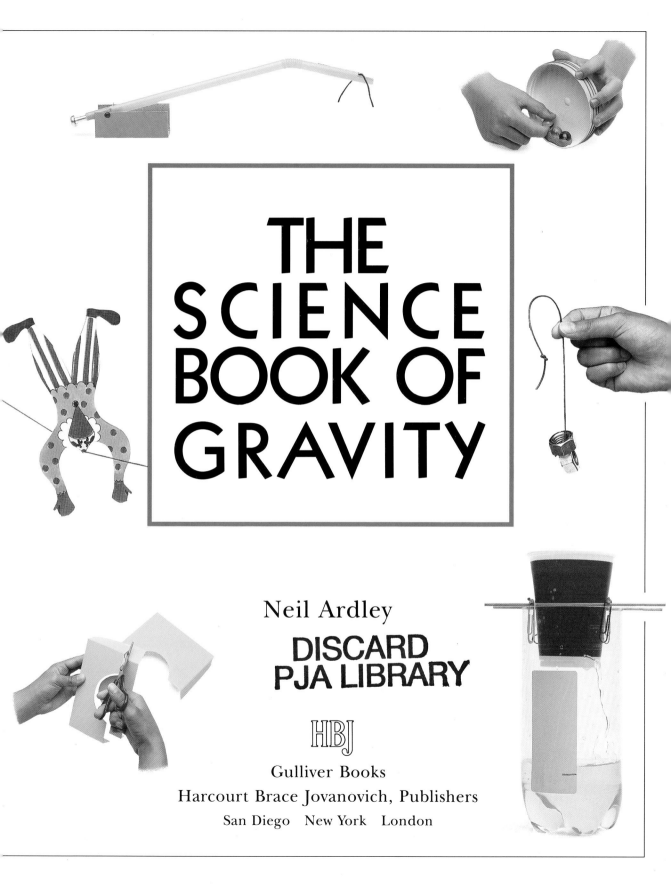

THE SCIENCE BOOK OF GRAVITY

Neil Ardley

HBJ

Gulliver Books

Harcourt Brace Jovanovich, Publishers

San Diego   New York   London

What is gravity?

When you jump up into the air, why do you fall back down again? You fall because of an invisible force called gravity. Gravity pulls objects toward one another. The strength of this pull depends on the amount of matter an object has—its "mass." The larger the object's mass, the greater the pull. The earth is very massive, and its gravity is very strong—it pulls everything on it toward its center, from the smallest animal to the tallest skyscraper.

High dive
When this diver leaps off the diving board, gravity pulls him faster and faster toward the pool below.

Watching your weight
Gravity pulls you downward with a certain amount of force. We call this amount your weight. You can measure it by standing on a scale.

Light work
Because the moon has less mass than the earth, its gravity is much weaker. Astronauts have only one-sixth of their normal weight when they are on the moon.

Star systems

Gravity makes the planets orbit the sun and even holds the stars together in immense groups called galaxies.

Down to earth

A parachute drops slowly because air pushes against it, opposing gravity.

Balancing act

A sea lion can balance a ball by keeping its nose under the ball's "center of gravity," or balancing point.

Pulling power

Everything has gravity—even an apple pulls with a small force. But the earth's pull is so much stronger that the apple falls to the ground.

⚠ This is a warning symbol. It appears within experiments next to steps that require caution. When you see this symbol, ask an adult for help.

Be a safe scientist
Follow all the instructions carefully and always use caution, especially with glass, scissors, matches, or sharp objects. Never put anything in your mouth or eyes.

Be careful when you drop, roll, or throw things. When testing gravity, do not throw things down or push them down slopes. Just let them drop or roll naturally.

The harder they fall

Does a heavy object fall faster than a light object? Try dropping two balls—a light one and a heavy one— and see which ball lands first.

You will need:

Ball bearing

Light plastic ball

Cookie sheet

Modeling clay

Rolling pin

Make sure your hands are level when you drop the balls.

1 Weigh the two balls in your hands. The ball bearing should feel heavier. Put the cookie sheet on the ground.

2 Hold the two balls above the cookie sheet. Release them both at exactly the same time. Listen—they hit the cookie sheet at the same time.

3 Roll out some clay.

Because the acceleration of gravity is constant, the balls fall at the same speed. But the heavier ball falls with greater force.

4 Place the clay on the cookie sheet. Drop the two balls again.

The ball bearing makes the deepest impression because gravity pulls on it with the strongest force.

5 Carefully lift the balls to see which one has made the deepest impression in the clay.

Make sure the clay is smooth.

Air lift
Very light objects, such as these dandelion seeds, fall slowly or even float through the air. They are so light that the air holds them up, working against the force of gravity.

Hit the spot

Release some balls at the top of a chute and try to guess exactly where they will land. Will balls of different sizes land in different places?

You will need:

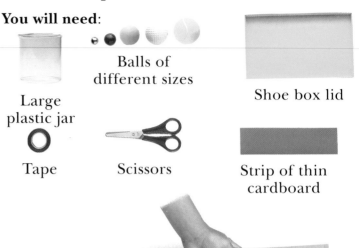

Large plastic jar

Balls of different sizes

Shoe box lid

Tape

Scissors

Strip of thin cardboard

Make one piece longer than the other.

1 Cut the shoe box lid into two pieces. Then cut a half-circle out of each piece.

2 Cut tabs in each end of the strip of cardboard

3 Fold back the tabs and tape them to the two parts of the lid to make a chute.

4 Set the support high up on a box or table. Release a ball at the top of the chute. Place the jar where the ball lands.

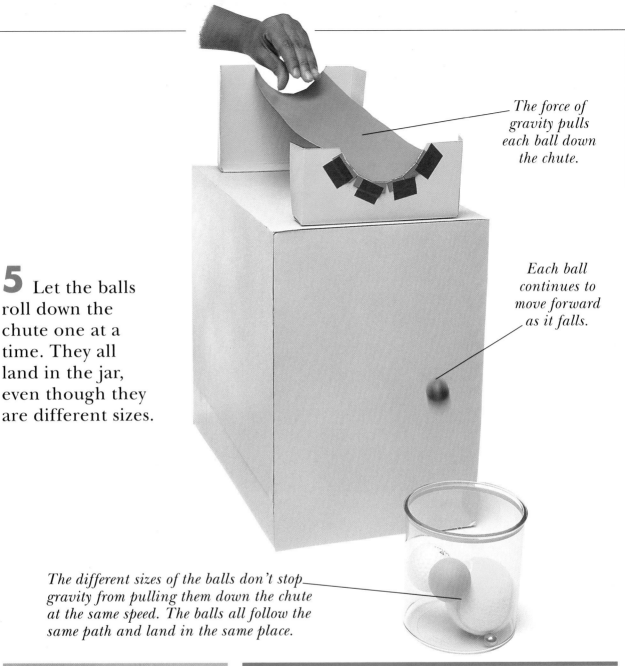

The force of gravity pulls each ball down the chute.

Each ball continues to move forward as it falls.

5 Let the balls roll down the chute one at a time. They all land in the jar, even though they are different sizes.

The different sizes of the balls don't stop gravity from pulling them down the chute at the same speed. The balls all follow the same path and land in the same place.

Skis in the sky
Pulled by gravity, a ski jumper races down a steep chute into the air. The skier's high speed carries him forward as he drops, making a long jump.

Ramp racer

Race a car down a ramp from different heights and see how gravity controls its speed. Gravity makes objects move faster the farther they fall.

You will need:

Scissors

Shoe box with lid

Toy car

Each slot should reach halfway across the end.

Cut the slot on the opposite side of the slots in the box.

Cut into the corner to open out the lid.

1 Cut away most of one end and one side of the shoe box. Cut three slots in the end that is left.

2 Cut the lid to the same width as the side of the box. Cut a slot halfway across one end. This is your ramp.

Gravity pulls the car down the ramp. It gains speed and travels a short distance.

3 Fit the ramp into the bottom slot of the box. Hold the toy car at the top of the ramp and then release it.

4 Fit the ramp into the middle slot and release the car again. This time it moves faster and travels farther.

The ramp is higher, so the car gains more speed.

5 Fit the ramp into the top slot. Now the car races down the ramp and travels a long way.

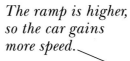

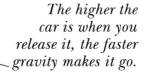

The higher the car is when you release it, the faster gravity makes it go.

Hold on tight!

The cars on this roller coaster have no motors—gravity alone propels them around the track. Beginning with a fast drop down a steep ramp gives the cars enough speed for the rest of the ride.

Simple swinger

Set a pendulum swinging and see if each swing takes the same amount of time. What happens if you change the weight and length of the pendulum?

You will need:

Tape

Three large
metal nuts

String

Scissors

Stopwatch, or watch
with second hand

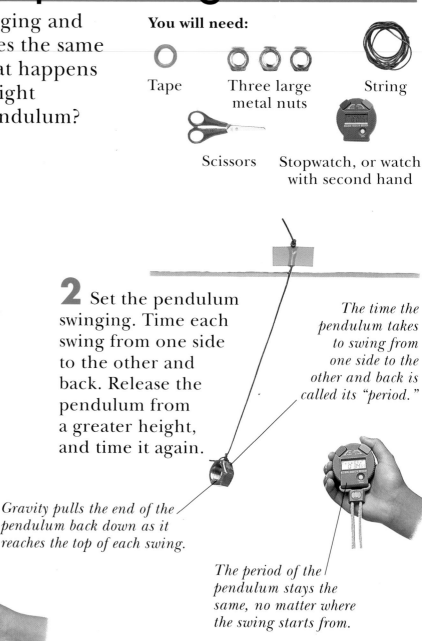

1 Cut two different lengths of string. Tie a metal nut to each. These are your pendulums. Tape the shorter pendulum to a support, such as the edge of a table.

2 Set the pendulum swinging. Time each swing from one side to the other and back. Release the pendulum from a greater height, and time it again.

The time the pendulum takes to swing from one side to the other and back is called its "period."

Gravity pulls the end of the pendulum back down as it reaches the top of each swing.

The period of the pendulum stays the same, no matter where the swing starts from.

3 Make the pendulum heavier by adding an extra metal nut.

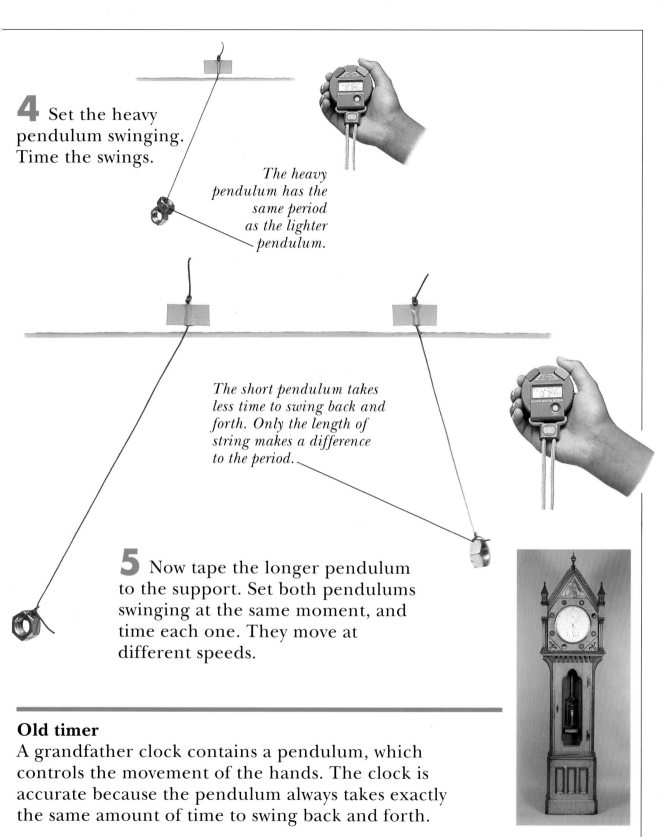

4 Set the heavy pendulum swinging. Time the swings.

The heavy pendulum has the same period as the lighter pendulum.

The short pendulum takes less time to swing back and forth. Only the length of string makes a difference to the period.

5 Now tape the longer pendulum to the support. Set both pendulums swinging at the same moment, and time each one. They move at different speeds.

Old timer

A grandfather clock contains a pendulum, which controls the movement of the hands. The clock is accurate because the pendulum always takes exactly the same amount of time to swing back and forth.

Water clock

Do you know how to measure time with falling water? Build a simple water clock. It works because gravity makes water fall at a regular rate.

You will need:

Four paper clips

Plastic cup

Water

Clear plastic bottle

Four thin wooden sticks

Adhesive label

Pen

Stopwatch, or watch with second hand

Hook the paper clips over the sticks and onto the bottle edge.

1 ⚠ Ask an adult to cut the top off the bottle. Then make a small hole near the base of the cup with one of the wooden sticks.

2 Make a support by attaching the wooden sticks to the top of the bottle with the paper clips as shown.

3 Make a mark on the label and attach it to the side of the bottle. Fill the bottle up to the mark.

4 Put the cup in the support. Fill the cup with water. Start the stopwatch as you begin pouring.

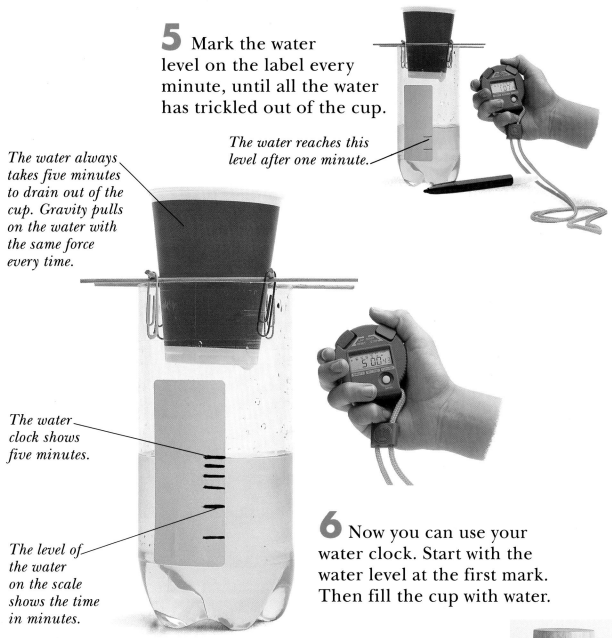

5 Mark the water level on the label every minute, until all the water has trickled out of the cup.

The water reaches this level after one minute.

The water always takes five minutes to drain out of the cup. Gravity pulls on the water with the same force every time.

The water clock shows five minutes.

The level of the water on the scale shows the time in minutes.

6 Now you can use your water clock. Start with the water level at the first mark. Then fill the cup with water.

Sands of time

This egg timer measures the time it takes to boil an egg. It contains an amount of sand that always takes three minutes to fall from the top chamber into the bottom chamber. To start the egg timer, you just turn it upside down.

Balancing act

Gravity seems to pull an object downward from just one point—its "center of gravity." Balancing an uneven shape is easy when you find this point.

You will need:

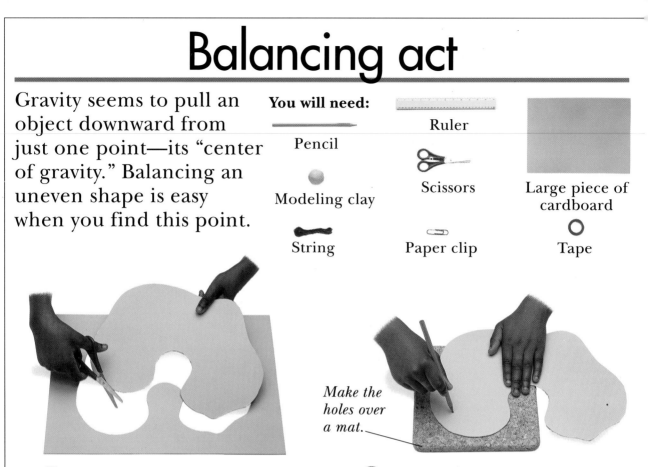

Ruler

Pencil

Modeling clay

Scissors

Large piece of cardboard

String

Paper clip

Tape

1 Cut out an uneven shape from the cardboard.

Make the holes over a mat.

2 Using the point of the pencil, make two small holes on opposite edges of the shape.

3 Now make a plumb line. Tie a loop in one end of the string and wrap a lump of clay around the other end.

4 Unbend the paper clip to form a hook. Tape it to the edge of a table. Hang the shape and then the plumb line on the hook.

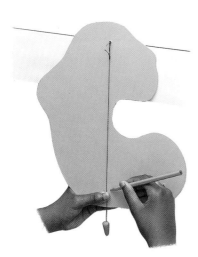

5 When the line stops moving, mark an **X** near where it crosses the edge of the shape.

6 Take the shape off the hook and draw a line between the **X** and the hole. Hang the shape from the other hole and repeat steps 4 to 6.

The point at which the two lines cross is the shape's center of gravity.

When gravity pulls down equally on all parts of the shape around its center of gravity, the shape balances.

On the beam
This gymnast keeps her balance while performing difficult exercises by making sure her center of gravity stays directly above the beam.

7 Place the shape on your finger at the point where the two lines cross. The shape balances.

Clowning around

Make a clown that can balance upside down on a high wire and never fall off! All you have to do is get the clown's center of gravity under the wire.

You will need:

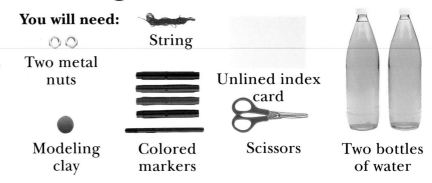

String

Two metal nuts

Modeling clay

Colored markers

Unlined index card

Scissors

Two bottles of water

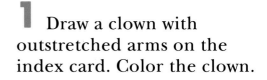

1 Draw a clown with outstretched arms on the index card. Color the clown.

2 Cut out the clown and make a small notch in its nose.

3 Stick a metal nut behind each of the clown's hands with some clay.

4 Tie the string to the necks of the bottles. Move the bottles apart to make a high wire.

5 Set the clown on the string so that it rests on the notch in its nose. The clown balances. Push it gently. It swings back and forth but does not fall.

Most of the clown's weight is in the heavy metal nuts at the ends of its arms.

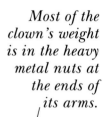

The clown cannot fall because its center of gravity, which is under the string, pulls it down onto the string.

Standing steady
Television cameras need to stay steady. This one is on a weighted stand, which gives it a low center of gravity, so that it will not wobble or tip over easily.

Uphill battle

Can a wheel roll uphill? It can if you make its center of gravity fall as the wheel rises.

You will need:

Marbles   Round lid   Piece of cardboard

Modeling clay   Rubber bands

1 Space the rubber bands evenly around the lid.

Place the marbles next to each other.

2 Stick the marbles to the inside edge of the lid with clay. This is your wheel.

Make sure the marbles are at the top of the wheel, facing up the ramp.

The wheel's center of gravity is in the heaviest part of the wheel—the marbles.

Gravity pulls the marbles down as low as possible.

3 Fold the cardboard to make a ramp. Put the wheel at the bottom of the ramp.

4 Release the wheel. It rolls up the ramp and stops near the top.

Not a pushover
This wobbly toy has a heavy base. When you tip it over, gravity makes it roll upright again.

Funny flier

Have fun trying to catch a balloon that refuses to fly straight! Its center of gravity moves around as it flies through the air, making it wobble.

You will need:

Water

Balloon pump

Two balloons

1 Pour some water into one of the balloons and tie a knot in the neck.

2 Push the water-filled balloon into the other balloon, then blow it up and tie the neck.

The balloon's center of gravity is in the water-filled balloon.

The balloon wobbles because its center of gravity changes as it moves.

3 Throw the balloon to a friend. It wobbles so much, it's almost impossible to catch!

Super balance

Tiny things might feel weightless in your hand, but gravity gives everything weight. Make a sensitive balance that can detect the weight of even the lightest objects.

You will need:

Ruler

Cardboard strip

Pin

Flexible drinking straw

Scissors

Screw

Pencil

Pieces of thread

Empty matchbox

Modeling clay

1 Push some clay into the long end of the straw. Then twist the screw into the clay.

2 Cut a notch in the short end of the straw.

3 ⚠ Push the pin through the straw near the screw.

4 Cut the outside part of the matchbox in half. This is the balance's support.

5 Use the ruler to draw a scale on the cardboard strip. Then bend the strip and stand it up behind the notched end of the straw.

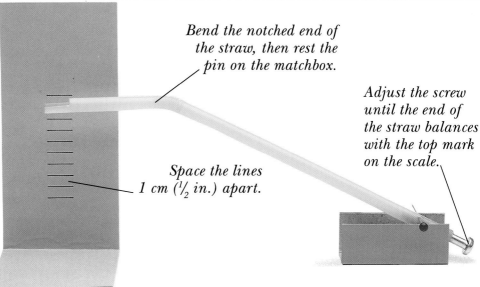

Bend the notched end of the straw, then rest the pin on the matchbox.

Adjust the screw until the end of the straw balances with the top mark on the scale.

Space the lines 1 cm ($\frac{1}{2}$ in.) apart.

6 This is your balance. Gently place a piece of thread on the notched end of the straw. The straw tips and moves down the scale.

The thread makes this end of the balance slightly heavier. Gravity pulls it so that the straw tilts.

The weight of an object is the force with which gravity pulls on it.

Weight check

Scientists use very sensitive weighing machines to measure small amounts of chemicals and medicines. A weighing machine like this one is so accurate that it can measure weight to within one ten-thousandth of a gram.

Weight lifter

The earth's gravity pulls on everything, but some forces work against it. See how water pushes up against objects and makes them seem less heavy.

You will need:

Two paper clips

Scissors

Tape

Water

Modeling clay

Tall, clear container

Four rubber bands

Knitting needle

Two full jars of equal weight

1 Loop a short rubber band around each jar. Unbend the paper clips and hook them under the rubber bands.

Cover the sharp end of the needle with clay.

Hang one jar inside the container.

2 Rest the knitting needle across the top of the container. Hang both jars from the needle with rubber bands.

3 Tape the needle firmly to the container.

Both jars hang at the same height because they weigh the same.

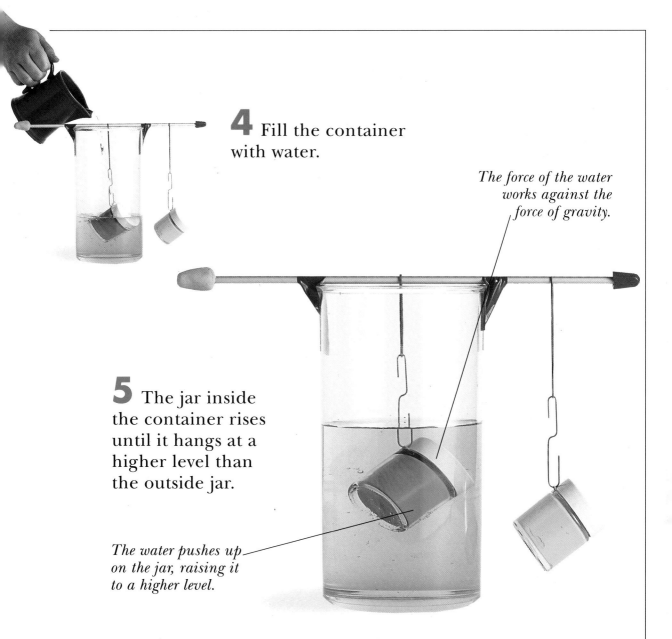

4 Fill the container with water.

The force of the water works against the force of gravity.

5 The jar inside the container rises until it hangs at a higher level than the outside jar.

The water pushes up on the jar, raising it to a higher level.

Lighter logs

It is hard to move these heavy logs on land. That's why they are moved on water. The water works against the pull of gravity, pushing the logs up and making them easier to move.

Odd bottle

Defy gravity by stopping water from falling through the holes in the base of a bottle. It's easy to do if you use air pressure.

You will need:

Scissors

Water

Bowl

Plastic bottle with screw-on cap

1 ⚠ Ask an adult to make several holes in the base of the bottle with the scissors.

2 Stand the bottle in the bowl and quickly fill it with water. Screw the cap on right away.

Hold the bottle by the cap and do not squeeze the sides.

3 Lift the bottle. No water flows out of the holes.

Air beneath the bottle pushes up against the holes. It works against the force of gravity and stops the water from falling.

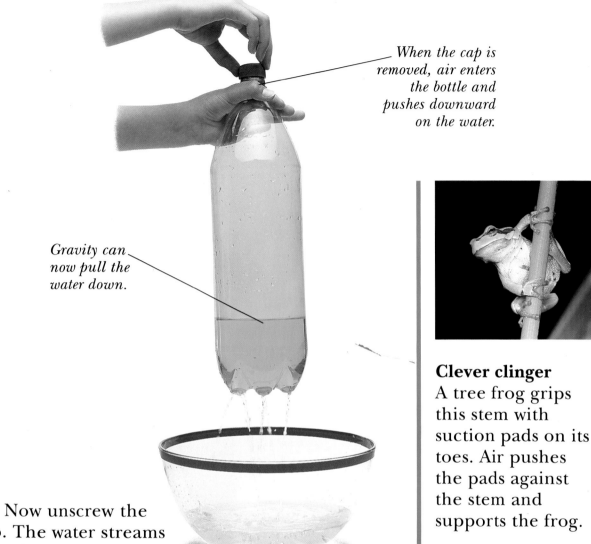

When the cap is removed, air enters the bottle and pushes downward on the water.

Gravity can now pull the water down.

4 Now unscrew the cap. The water streams out of the bottle.

Clever clinger
A tree frog grips this stem with suction pads on its toes. Air pushes the pads against the stem and supports the frog.

Picture credits
(Picture credits abbreviation key: B=below, C=center, L=left, R=right, T=top)

Allsport: 6TL, 7TL, 19BR; Bridgeman Art Library: 15BR; J. Allan Cash: 21BL; Colorsport: 11BL; Pete Gardner: 22BL; The Image Bank/Guido A. Rossi: 27BR; Frank Lane/HD Brand: 29BR; NASA/Science Photo Library: 6TR, 7TR; Planet Earth Pictures/Mike Coltman: 7CR; Pictor International: 9BR, 13BR; Tim Ridley: 7BL, 17BR; Science Photo Library/David Leah: 25BR

Picture research Clive Webster

Science consultant Jack Challoner

Additional photography Dave King and Tim Ridley

Dorling Kindersley would like to thank Jenny Vaughan for editorial assistance; Basi! Snook for supplying toys; Mrs Bradbury, Mr Millington, the staff and children of Allfarthing Junior School, Wandsworth, especially Hannah Carey, Richard Clenshaw, Nadeen Flower, Alex MacDougald, Keisha McLeod, Kemi Owoturo, Casston Rogers-Brown, Ben Sells, Cheryl Smith, and Michael Spencer.

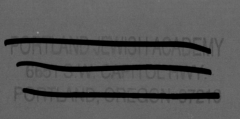